PRAISE

"*Stay Until Tomorrow* is a debut book full of courage, resilience, insight, and the poet's deep capacity for love. These poems, conversational in nature, are profoundly healing for survivors and shine necessary light into the dark places."

—Diana Whitney, poet, editor, and author of *Dark Beds*

"Meghan Wentworth's poetry is poignant and evocative, exploring themes of growth and connection, the pull between self-reliance and dependence, and survival in the face of trauma and loss. I found myself immersed in the raw honesty of poems such as 'Secret Garden,' 'Peirce Island,' and 'Him.' Wentworth's verse invites all readers to inhabit profoundly personal spaces of memory, isolation, and confrontation, thereby sparking reflection on how we process our own similar life challenges."

—Emily M. Hinnov, PhD, professor of English and program coordinator at Great Bay Community College and editor-in-chief of *The Heron*

Stay Until Tomorrow

Stay Until Tomorrow ©2024 Meghan A. Patricia Wentworth
Release Date: April 4, 2025
All Rights Reserved.

Printed in the USA. First printing.

Published by Rootstock Publishing
an imprint of Ziggy Media LLC
Montpelier, Vermont 05602
info@rootstockpublishing.com
www.rootstockpublishing.com

Paperback ISBN: 978-1-57869-188-3
eBook ISBN: 978-1-57869-189-0
Library of Congress Number: 2024925961

Book design by Eddie Vincent, ENC Graphic Services.
Cover photo courtesy of the author.

No part of this book may be reproduced or transmitted in any form or by any means whatsoever without express written permission from the publisher, except in the case of brief quotations embodied in critical articles and reviews. For reprint permission, email info@rootstockpublishing.com.

For permissions or to schedule a reading, contact the author at mapknow@gmail.com.

Stay Until Tomorrow

poems

by
Meghan A. Patricia Wentworth

Montpelier, VT

Dear Reader,

Each one of these poems captures an important moment in my life. These moments shaped who I am as a person and led me to do what I do. They drove me to my breaking point and occasionally helped put me back together. The poems reveal secrets that I have let stew inside me. Secrets that keep me up at night and give me nightmares if I ever fall asleep. They are the skeletons that I can no longer keep in the closet.

My writing has been instrumental in my healing process. It has helped me deal with my stress, anxiety, and depression. It has helped me learn how to heal the "little Meghan" who lives in the garden behind my sternum. A place where she is safe and sound. Safe from those who have tried hard to destroy her. A place for her to finally grow in a sanctuary where all of her needs are met.

These poems explore my moments of love, pain, suffering, and self-healing. They illuminate the people who have been my light and others who have pulled me into the darkness.

It took me a long time to get where I am. To finally find comfort and to decide to share it all with you. I hope this book helps you feel validated and heard—and inspires you to believe that things can get better. Our experiences make us who we are and give us the opportunity to connect with others.

All of my light and love,
Meghan

For B, I am infected with you. Even if there were a cure, I wouldn't
take it. You make me stronger, healthier, and immune to
those who threaten to harm me.

For N, you live inside my bones. You give me structure, stability, and safety.
Will you come join me for a walk in the garden
that blooms in my rib cage?

And last but not least, OG. Every heartbeat is yours.
You are the very reason why I am still alive. I inhale and exhale for you.
You make me whole and unbroken.

Contents

Grieving in Silence 1
Center Stage 3
This House 4
Thirty Minutes 5
The Little Fox 7
London Boy 8
My Traveler 9
Third from the Left 10
Blue Razz Ice 12
22 13
Red Light/Green Light 14
Nariz Besos 15
15 Good Years Left 16
Boys Will Be Boys 17
Sapphire Girls 19
Sign Language and Sunblock 20
Jimmy and the Psych Ward Blizzards 21
Pity Parties 22
The Pods 23
Sunken Garden 25
Always 27
Lists 28
Episodes 29
Mexico 31
Capsized 32
Futon Mattress 33

Bird Watching 34
Don't Look Under the Bed 36
Age of Accountability 37
Cribbage 38
My Little Moose 39
Wal-Mart 40
Navy Man 42
Wallis Sands 44
Mount Vernon Variety 45
My Mother's Line 46
The First Sip 47
Happiness? 48
Venus de Milo 49
Birthday Balloons 50
Ruby Grapefruit 51
Her 53
An Education 54
"You're Ruining Your Life" 55
Family Ties 56
Latibule 57

About the Author 58
Acknowledgments 59

Grieving in Silence

"Yeah, well at least he wasn't really yours."
I hear it all the time.
Who wrote the rules on grieving?
Why is there a spectrum of loss?
We compare ourselves
like we have something to prove.
Your loss is somehow measured differently,
perceived as greater than mine.
Almost like I'm not worthy of tears,
like sadness is being wasted on me.
All I know is this:
when they put him in my arms
I could never imagine letting go.
Every giggle,
every smile,
every milestone reached—
all for me.
I'd leave the room
and he would follow.
First he'd crawl,
then he'd walk,
then he'd run to me.
"Momma"
is who I became.
For him. I'd wake
every morning to him laughing,
waiting for me to pick him up.
Soon the day would come
when we'd finally change his last name.
Instead I lie on the rug in the room
that was once in his nursery,
crying tears I shouldn't,
because he was never really mine.

Aching as I cling to the memory.
The memory of him.
The smell of his curls after a bath,
his big, beautiful brown eyes staring back into mine.
Sharing it with no one
while I drown on the floor in silence.

Center Stage

The lights are bright
but I am calm
because he is in this little playhouse with me.
Can a soulmate be your brother?
Together we make one complete person.
Our souls intertwine in a perfectly choreographed dance.
Step touch, step touch, step touch.
One foot in front of the other
as we walk hand-in-hand,
experiencing what no one else can grasp
or understand.
It's us against the world,
and nearly all the people in it.
Even when I am wrong,
he tells me I am right.
He will fight with me until he is covered in bruises
and his perfect ballet toes are broken.
He breaks for me.
He repairs himself with tape and glue
and gets back on stage with a smile on his face,
prepared for his next number.
I will be with him until the curtains are drawn,
every rose is thrown,
and all the encores are finished.

This House

This was the house of my dreams.
Every day I watched it being built from the ground up.
Every decision was mine,
from the color of the walls to the maple hardwood floors,
to the placement of every outlet.
It was mine,
my happiest of places.
Where they brought my son to me,
a little boy full of smiles and laughter.
Where for months and months I watched him grow.
Where he learned to walk,
learned to talk.
Where I started to feel him slowly slip away.
Where I had to begin to share him.
Where my marriage began to crumble.
Where a house became divided.
Where I returned in the middle of the night
wearing paper panties and paper clothes
after the assault that cracked my foundation.
Where after a year, they took my son
out of my arms with barely any notice.
Where I began to crumble.
Where I realized I was broken.
Where I returned again in paper panties and paper clothes
after deciding a knife to the throat was the only answer
to months of agony and torture.
This is where I was left in pieces
scattered across the perfect wooden floors.
Barely a resemblance to the sturdy foundation
poured just a year before.
This is where I had to say goodbye
to my happiest of places.
Where I must begin to build
myself from the ground up.

Thirty Minutes

I didn't file the report like I should have.
You can judge all you want,
but you are not me.
You will never understand.
You weren't on that couch.
Thirty minutes.
One half hour.
One thousand and eight hundred seconds.
That's how long it took him to greet me at the door,
casually rip my pants down, and shove himself
inside me.
Nothing a little spit can't fix, right?
Then straight to the emergency room I went.
"You can sit in the waiting room.
Someone will be with you shortly."
Shortly?
What is shortly?
Thirty minutes.
One half hour.
One thousand and eight hundred seconds
until pills, shots, and questions.
Knees bend and another unwanted object
is inside me. "Bruising, redness,
irritation, and abrasions," she whispers.
Left in paper panties and paper clothes,
feeling slightly more broken
than I had been hours before.
Number 9137.
The number is documented on my evidence box
and in my brain forever.
Thirty minutes.
One half hour.
One thousand and eight hundred seconds
spent recalling my story to the detective.

"It will come down to he said/she said.
Do you really want to go through with it?"
Thirty minutes always seemed
insignificant until now.

The Little Fox

I've been searching the skies
for quite some time, my darling.
Vulpecula and Anser,
the little fox and the goose.
I look up at them and think of him.
I would give them all to him,
every star in that constellation.
Not enough?
How about the sun?
The moon?
All of the stars
in every galaxy
in every universe?
I would bring them all back to him.
He could generate a supernova and it wouldn't matter.
I would still shine for him.
Am I bright enough?
Or am I nothing but a little stardust?

London Boy

He was incredibly charismatic.
Everyone was his best friend
but I was his favorite.
I would walk into a room, and he'd instantly
make me feel welcome,
like I belonged.
He'd give me a giant hug,
and we'd whisper the drama of the moment.
I felt comfort in his arms,
like nothing could hurt me
even when the world was crashing around me.
Why is London so far away?
I miss his quiet mannerisms and dry humor.
He could get me laughing
even on my saddest of days.
When will he be able to stay?
I need every holiday with him,
every Thanksgiving and Christmas,
every birthday celebration.
He needs to save me from the wild magpies.
I even want him on the regular days.
He tells me, "I'll meet you on the decks."

My Traveler

He explored me.
Every inch of me.
Like I was undiscovered land.
Like he was sent to claim me.
And I let him.
I would have let him forever.
We studied each other,
learning our twists and turns,
traveling a road I'd never been down
but was oh so eager to explore.
Tracing each borderline with our fingertips.
I needed him,
and he let me have him.
I can't believe I stumbled upon him.
My roads were crumbling
under the earthquake.
But I'd see him,
and the whole world would go away.
He helped put me back together
when everything was falling down.
It was just me and him.
Tucked away.
Tangled up in sheets.
I needed it for as long as I could have it.
Forever ended too soon.

I needed him,
and he let me have him.
There is still much left to discover.
So many maps to unfold,
roads to cross,
secret sites to uncover.
Will he come explore with me again?

Third from the Left

It started off as a whisper,
Third from the left.
I tried to shake it out of my mind
like erasing an old Etch a Sketch.
But it didn't work.
It grew louder and louder,
Third from the left.
Until it was all consuming
and became my every thought.
Over and over and over again,
Third from the left.
Soon I grew to like the idea,
started to repeat it like a new favorite song.
The melody was enticing,
Third from the left.
The idea grew clearer
until I was almost excited
by the mere thought of it.
Was today the day?
Leave work and drive home.
Walk upstairs.
Leave a note taped to the shelf in the entryway.
Go to the kitchen.
Grab my favorite knife,
Third from the left.
Unlock the back door.
Go into the bathroom.
Get into the bathtub.
Lie down by the faucet.
I wouldn't want to leave a mess.
Call 911.
Is today the day?
I couldn't get the song out of my head,

Third from the left.
Let me play it for you
so you will understand its beauty.
Listen to the melody
and let it wrap you in its warmth—
Third from the left.
Third from the left.
Third from the left.

Blue Razz Ice

I could tell what he was thinking by the look on his face.
His eyebrows would furrow when I made him laugh,
like he couldn't believe I'd said what I said.
My dark and dry sense of humor got him every time
as we lay in bed in that quaint, little hotel room.
His eyebrows always gave him away.
He'd take a hit of his Blue Razz Ice,
and I would taste it on my lips.
When did his eyebrows become unrecognizable?
When did he become a stranger,
some might even say a monster?
To me, he was never that.
He was someone I could have loved,
someone I would have loved to love.
But everything changed that one night in July.
All our plans could no longer come true.
Will his time locked away change his face?
Will I no longer recognize
my favorite feature on his perfect face?
What am I to do now?
Unable to fathom the news, I will forever
search the crowds for his captivating eyebrows.

22

Lana Elise.
I fell madly in love with the 21 who came before her.
Each one had a story and a name.
Never the same name twice.
How did they grow up?
I can picture their faces.
Leo Charles.
Hopes constantly built up, dreams endlessly dashed.
Forever waiting for her.
Henry Philip.
All the ones who came before her
and all the ones who came after.
Maxwell Robert.
Each took a little piece of my heart until there was barely
any muscle left.
How do I survive
when I don't have enough heart left to beat?
Then she came,
and the pieces started to stitch themselves together.
Every day I'm with her,
the rhythm gets stronger.
Thump thump. Thump thump. Thump thump.
My little Olivia Grace,
my heart will forever beat for you.

Red Light/Green Light

I didn't want to go grocery shopping
so my mom let me stay in the car,
counting down the minutes until we could go home.
I put my headphones in and started listening to my iPod Shuffle,
hoping she'd be back soon.
Then he drove by the parked car
like it was a regular Tuesday
and he'd finished getting food for his new family.
Like he didn't even know me
and didn't recognize her car,
the one he'd helped her pick out.
Before I could stop myself,
my hand was on the handle
and I stepped out of her pink Hyundai Accent.
I ran to his car where it had stopped at the red light.
I knew he'd be excited to see me.
Certainly, he wanted me.
It had been so long.
Too long.
I stood at his passenger door and leaned down to open it.
But as my hand reached the metal,
the light turned green
and he drove away.
Not even looking in his rearview mirror.
He drove away from me
like I was a panhandler he didn't know.
He had to get back to his family,
which wasn't me anymore.

Nariz Besos

The first time I told someone I loved them
and meant it, it was an easy love.
It came almost instantly.
I was young and reckless,
without a care in the world,
desperate for someone
to call my own.
Was it like that for him?
I feel like it was—
until it wasn't.
It stopped being simple.
My complications started to outweigh
what I could offer.
I would have given the world to him
if he had just asked.
I would have changed myself
to fit into his puzzle.
But my pieces were too big
and I hated having to make myself smaller.
It was him but it was also me.
It hurt at the time
but made sense in the end.
That purple dress was better off unworn.

15 Good Years Left

Our final phone call.
"I only have 15 good years left,"
he said over my speaker.
He didn't want to deal with me and my drama.
Fixing what he broke didn't seem worth it.
All I asked for was a little tape, a little glue.
But he let me go
like he let go of the other three.
How can his new family not see?
How are we the problem
when little by little,
he left all of us?
20 years ago.
8 years ago.
5 years ago.
4 months ago.
For various reasons,
but it all came down to one common denominator: him.
It always came down and came back to him.
He didn't want to repair the four of us.
He didn't want to work on a problem he didn't see.
I thought he could at least make an exception for me.
I was, after all, his little goldmine.
The secret weapon.
The one he loved the most.
I was the last one standing,
but it's almost as if I never existed.
Red light, green light,
I was back at that stoplight,
begging for him to let me in.
But he drove away from me for the last time.
He never even looked in the rearview mirror.

Boys Will Be Boys

I'm going to spoil you.
You'll stay single forever.
Damn, I was kind of hoping
when I came back in, your shirt would be off.
No, I don't have any expectations.
I just want you to be comfortable.
You don't get what guys need.
Are you seriously going to make me wait
after I've already had it?
Mommy milkers.
Do you feel like sucking dick tonight?
Deleted... I swear!
20 bucks says you don't know who this is.
Good luck finding anyone to stick around.
Are you single?
Damn, look at your boobs.
You should really be taking anything you can get, tbh.
You're so incredibly, deliciously sexual looking.
Your glasses are sexy AF, btw.
Isn't this what you wanted?
I bet you're a good girl.
How long did you breastfeed for?
I love you.
Are you seriously not gonna let me hit that?
You're wearing too many layers.
Honestly, I don't give a shit.
You do you, girl.
Get over here, you owe me.
I'll pay for you to get a pedicure.
Can I cum on your glasses?
If you don't suck my dick, I'm not coming over.
Yes, you can keep going.
I'll give you a facial.

You nagging me for it is very unattractive.
Bend over so I can see what I'm working with.
Nothing will ever be good enough for you.
I don't drive to pussy, pussy drives to me.
You're such a prude.
I feel like I just made love to you.
Do I have to be nice?
Or is degrading fine?
That's way more fun.

Sapphire Girls

Her three perfect girls.
The Sapphire girls.
Our cut and clarity were flawless.
She shaped us into an image that fit her lifestyle,
just enough to please her
but not too much to rub her the wrong way.
I tried to be the perfect gem, her perfect stone,
but somewhere along the way, I began to crumble.
I couldn't be shiny and new for her.
I stumbled and tumbled from the top of her mountain.
And when she finally saw me,
she tossed me aside like a pebble caught in her shoe.
No longer worthy.
No longer precious.
I was no longer
her Sapphire girl.
But was I ever truly valued?
Or was I a piece of jewelry she'd reluctantly inherited
and was more than eager to regift.
Maybe she'll be satisfied with her other two Sapphire girls.
Maybe she was never meant to have a third.

Sign Language and Sunblock

They tried to tell her, but she couldn't understand.
They came to the door in a panic.
They were signing too fast, and she couldn't comprehend.
They tried to save me, but they failed.
I pretended I didn't know what they were talking about,
pretended they were crazy, and nothing had happened.
I stood on the table and told her
she should continue applying my sunblock,
so I could go out and play.
Maybe if I'd let them explain it slowly,
or even had them write it down,
she would have understood,
and I'd be safe and protected.
But I couldn't let her know the secret.
Would she even believe it
or would it get me in trouble?
The rollercoaster in my stomach told me to keep it quiet.
No one had to know about the lifted dresses.
The abuse on the playground.
The touches under the bed.
If I'd said something, would it have changed things?
Could I have protected myself and them?
The thought keeps me up at night—
all the broken boys and girls who could have been saved
if only I'd spilled my secrets.

Jimmy and the Psych Ward Blizzards

I met up with him on the inside.
I saw the star tattoo on the side of his neck
the day we met
that first night in the pods.
He recognized me almost immediately.
We were always together for the rest of my time.
He was my rock in an unknown world.
It's a different type of disorientation
on the inside.
You don't know the time,
you don't have a phone,
or any way to connect to the outside world.
But I had Jimmy and he grounded me.
In the scariest moments of my life, he was there.
He taught me how to navigate the environment.
My favorite part was a dessert
I dubbed "The Psych Ward Blizzard."
Milk.
Vanilla Ice Cream.
Crushed Graham Crackers.
Mix them together and call yourself Betty Crocker.
It was the little things that brought me back to reality,
grounded me when my head was hazy.
I needed Jimmy and I needed those Blizzards.
Every night we'd play cards or trivia and eat those Blizzards,
all while being watched like we were lab rats.
Every fifteen minutes.
We were watched constantly,
and checked on and recorded.
There were so many rules to follow
I could barely keep track.
But Jimmy was always there to help me.

Pity Parties

"Pity parties are for children."
Why not just sharpen my knife now?
I'm almost there.
I'm hanging off the edge.
Even a light breeze would send me over,
not to mention a conversation like this.
Is this love?
It doesn't seem like real love.
It seems like the love I'm used to, though.
A little gaslighting,
a little judgment.
Put me down just enough
for me to almost give up,
then at the last minute
extend a hand to pull me up.
The games.
I could go on and on about the games,
but I don't want to play anymore.
Take all of my poker chips.
Her hand is better than mine
and always has been.
I hope I was a worthy adversary,
but we both know
I could never beat her.
I never see the moves coming.
She will outsmart me every time.

The Pods

I had to go in, even though I didn't want to.
The song was on repeat, and I couldn't stop it.
The lyrics flowed so beautifully,
I didn't want the music to stop.
Third from the left.
I wanted to.
I really wanted to.
Today was the day,
and the idea made me happier than I'd been in months.
But wait.
Should I tell someone?
Should I divulge my plans?
I called my therapist and she told me to go.
I needed to go or she'd take matters into her own hands,
and it was better if I went willingly.
So I did.
She called my mom to come get me, and I left.
I had a plan, but she was ruining my plan.
I walked into the waiting room, and almost immediately
they sent me to the back.
Question after question.
Blood draws and urine samples,
paper panties and paper clothes.
I was escorted by a nurse and security guard
to the back of the house.
This was the room before the room.
The pods, as they called them.
No one told me about the pods.
No one told me anything.
For hours and hours and hours I waited.
Not a word from anyone,
just people crying in the other rooms.
Screams and cries and confusion.

I had to pee in a bathroom with half a door.
They were always watching
my every move.
I tried to leave but they wouldn't let me.
I had to stay in an eight-foot by six-foot room
with only my thoughts to keep me company.
Then he came.
He walked by my open door and said
"This place fucking sucks."
He couldn't have been more right.
I asked if we were allowed to be friends
and offered him half my sandwich.
He'd been here for days with nothing to eat.
But before long they took me away
to the room after the room,
where I stayed for days and days and days
and tried to make the song go away.
Third from the left.
I don't think it will ever go away,
but hopefully one day I can get the music to stop.

Sunken Garden

We were growing together
right from our roots.
Our seeds were planted side by side
and our tangled stems grew
up towards the sunlight,
thriving in all seasons—
even ones we thought we wouldn't survive.
We still grew,
always upwards.
Showing off our beautiful petals,
basking in the sunlight.
But soon the weather turned
and it began to change us.
The winters were harsher,
and the summers withered our leaves brown.
Spring wasn't as prosperous as we'd hoped.
More plants sprung up in our garden.
Seemingly dainty crocuses.
A beautiful but invasive plant.
I was plucked and trimmed and pruned
but I survived.
The crocuses were cut down
but their roots remained.
We did our best to grow over them.
One day, they might even be forgotten,
especially when we planted another seed.
Surely this new blossom would make our garden thrive.
And it did, for a time.
He grew beautifully.
I gave him my sunlight,
and when the autumn rain came,
I made sure he was never thirsty.
But he was meant for another garden,

one with less weeds.
Soon after he left, I began to shrink and shrivel.
My petals started to fall
one by one.
I untangled our stems.
I could no longer grow.
It wasn't my garden anymore.
I was ripped out by my roots
and left on the cobblestone path,
wilting in the summer sun.
A small piece of the garden I once inhabited,
plucked and trimmed and pruned.

Always

She is always the version I need her to be.
She changes herself to fit into my puzzle.
Friend, therapist, listener,
or just Aunt.
Especially when I need a distraction.
She knows what to say,
even when I don't want her to say it.
She keeps me grounded
when I feel like I can't come down.
When the anxiety takes over, she is always
one second away from saving me.
She's taught me to see a situation from the other side
and to realize maybe I'm not always right.
Maybe.
But still.
She is there, cheering me on and giving me guidance.
Even from miles away, she is with me.
Every time I go to the beach,
or have a big decision to make,
or I'm reading *the Goblet of Fire*
she is there.
Putting my edge pieces together,
and filling in the middle ones.
Always.

Lists

We sat there.
On her mattress on the floor.
Let's make a list,
she'd say,
of all the ways to make him stay.
Always go with him on errands.

She tapped the pen on the pad of paper.

What else?
Wild Horsey?
I suggested.
Yes, that would certainly work.
I would go
wherever he would go.
He couldn't leave us *with me there.*
That would be impossible.
But I didn't fit into his new puzzle,
his other lifestyle.
His other life.
So we'd sit
and make lists.
Surely there was something we hadn't thought of.
Something that *I* hadn't thought of.
Couldn't I be the reason for him to stay?
Wasn't it my job to make him stay?

Would he stay until tomorrow?

Episodes

It always felt like a strange way to say it—
episodes—
like it was a new television program.
Well, it must have been entertaining to watch
from the outside.
But inside the house?
A completely different story.
When an episode would start,
I'd lock myself in the bathroom
or run upstairs to my room.
Our room.
I would sit and wait
for it to be over.
I never knew how long it would last.
Sometimes I'd get tricked
with pleading at the door.
"Please, please, please."
"It's okay."
"I'm okay."
But it never was.
I'd get taken.
And thrown.
And scratched.
And beaten.
But we acted like this was fine.
Inside these walls,
we were a happy family.
We'd smile at the camera
and put the image in a frame.
I'd be good.
I'd be perfect.
But the episodes always came,
time and time and time again.

How long could we pretend
that this was normal?
That I was worth saving?
But the show never stopped.
It played over and over.
Even now,
when I close my eyes,
I'm right back behind that locked bathroom door.
About to open it up.

Mexico

I pretend I don't know where we went wrong.
But that's a lie—
I can name the day and time,
almost the minute.
I couldn't go to Mexico,
and he didn't understand why.
I didn't go.
I didn't show up for him.
Until then, he'd always show up for me.
I let him down.
Our flight has been delayed.
Even now, we're distant,
forced.
It doesn't feel like it did then.
Can we go back?
Can I get on that plane?
Can I show up for him?
Maybe someday I'll get a boarding pass.
Until then, we can discuss the weather,
the time difference between us,
how the family is doing.
The little unimportant things.
Someday I'll get on that plane
and fly back to him.
Will he meet me at the airport?

Capsized

She came in less like a wave
and more like a storm.
We crashed on the rocks
but we survived.
I was her boat,
and she was my anchor.
I needed her,
and she needed me.
We weathered every storm
and basked in every beautiful, sunny day.
The water was iridescent,
shining just for us.
But soon we began to drift.
We couldn't see the shore.
I kept steering south,
but she wanted to go north.
I don't want to let her go,
but we can't continue to sail together.
Can we?
I will forever be tethered to her
but for now, I will let her
step into her own boat
and sail away from me.
But I can't wait
to set sail with her again.

Futon Mattress

It happened during *Garden State*.
It wasn't particularly good,
but then again
I didn't have anything to compare it to.
I had almost all my firsts with him.
Did he know?
Does he regret it
like I regret it?
On the floor.
In his empty room.
On a futon mattress.
We continued
for years.
He'd call me in the middle of the night
and I'd come right over.
Sneak in and sneak out
as if I was never there.
I was his secret,
and he kept me on the floor
on that futon mattress.
When she came,
he didn't tell me about her.
He kept me his secret
and I didn't know until the very end.
Until I was done being a secret.
I regret a lot of things,
but especially what we did to her.
Unknowingly or not.
I regret him
and that old, musky futon mattress.

Bird Watching

We both know what you did to me.
It went on for years.
No words will heal it.
But I don't need words,
I have my memories.
You have them, too.
Do they flash in your mind
on the nights you can't sleep?
Do they haunt you
or do you pretend it didn't happen?
Do you think your mind
is playing tricks on you?
Slowly I erase the memories
to create new ones
you aren't a part of.
Memories you won't experience
because I finally chose what was best for me.
I put myself first.
You can say and do
and think and threaten
anything you want.
But it no longer has a hold on me.
I have let you go.
You can't hurt me anymore.
You're a distant memory
from a life I lived years ago.
I can barely remember our last conversation
or the one before that.
It's almost like you don't exist.
But now you decide to pay attention,
looking in from a distance.
You can watch me all you want.
I'll let you borrow my binoculars.

Zoom in.
That's as close as you're ever going to get.

Don't Look Under the Bed

It was always under the bed.
I can't tell you why.
A safe place?
Somewhere they would never look?
Just like we were playing
hide and seek.
But he always found me.
It comes back in clips.
Bits and pieces.
Flashes of memory.
I know there is more
that my brain refuses to share.
When I lay in bed awake at night,
I close my eyes and try to force
my brain to release its secrets.
But it keeps them locked up
in a cabinet
I can never open.
But still, I lie there trying.
What happened after I left
that small space?
What won't my brain show me?
Just flashes and bits and pieces.
Of me.
Of him.
Under his bed.
Unable to leave.
Still on a loop in my mind.

Age of Accountability

When do actions start to have consequences?
An alarm clock rings,
and then it begins.
Is it when you confess your sins?
Or when you say your Hail Marys
and are forgiven for your indiscretions?
It didn't start at five
when I swallowed all those pills.
It didn't start at ten
when I was beaten and left on the floor,
blood dripping from scratches on my throat.
It didn't start at thirteen
when my head was slammed into the keyboard
so hard the keys were dislodged.
It didn't start at seventeen
when I was told to ask Santa for a gun for Christmas
so I could kill myself.
It wasn't twenty-two
when I was beaten in the driveway
as onlookers stood frozen.
It wasn't at twenty-five
when my pain was not validated or offered an apology,
just met with information
saved for the right moment,
calculated for the satisfaction
of breaking me one final time.
I thought at thirty-five the alarm clock would ring,
and actions would start to have consequences,
but I was mistaken.

Cribbage

I let her beat me sometimes.
We'd sit at the table and play for hours.
I would count on my fingers,
and she would laugh and shake her head
while sipping her too-cold coffee.
She was a good teacher.
She taught me more than she ever knew,
cribbage being one of the lessons.
Our favorite game.
I couldn't wait
for my chance to play her again.
I would clear part of my workday
just to be with her.
We'd get out her cards
or take a long walk around the building,
talking and joking and speaking French.
I'd speak it poorly
just to get a rise out of her.
Not that I was that great to begin with,
but I loved to hear her laugh.
In the garden, we'd prune
and water her flowers.
We collected tomatoes
and ate them in the sunlight.
She brought light to even my darkest days.
She will forever be with me.
In the gardenias,
in the perfect cribbage hand,
and in the sunlight.
Always in the sunlight.

My Little Moose

He came so quickly.
They brought him to my arms
like they were dropping off a package.
I didn't know I could open up like this.
My heart didn't even skip a beat.
I knew he was mine from the moment
we got the call.
Two days later,
he appeared at our doorstep.
He fit into our family
like he'd been here all along,
cohesive in the chaos.
They gave us all the paperwork.
All we had to do was wait.
Wait for it to be finalized.
Wait for him to be truly ours.
Until then, we watched him grow
and learn
and walk
and talk.
Hoping the day would come.
But it never came,
and we had to let him go.
My little Moose.
They came back to our doorstep
and took him out of my arms.
Like the post office
had made a mistake.
Return to sender.

Wal-Mart

I'm used to people asking questions.
After all, we don't look the same.
She doesn't have my eyes
or my hair
or my complexion,
but that doesn't make her any less mine.
"Are you her nanny?"
I get that a lot.
Most of the time, I just brush off their curiosities,
make a joke or politely respond.
"She's so beautiful."
"Are you her babysitter?"
"No, I'm her mom,"
I say as I unload my groceries.
They exchange looks.
I can feel them watching us
as I continue checking out.
Then the whispers come,
if you can call them whispers.
"How is it possible?"
"I just have to say it, she's way too ugly to be her mom."
They both laugh.
I do my best to act like I don't hear.
Like their words don't pierce me.
Like I don't think that all the time.
So I do what I always do.
I smile at the cashier,
take my bags,
and leave with my beautiful baby girl,
who is all mine.
Even though we don't look the same,
and she doesn't have my eyes
or my hair

or my complexion.
She is all mine.

Navy Man

Was it all in my head?
Everyone acts like it is,
but it doesn't feel that way.
It certainly didn't feel that way
on the last night here,
before he left for training.
He stayed over,
and we drank Jameson straight.
When we kissed goodbye in the morning,
it felt like a dream I didn't want to wake up from.
When he left, we decided to keep in touch.
I know everyone says that,
but our emails back and forth burned with intensity.
Pages and pages and pages of emails.
It was almost like he never left.
Deep discussions,
funny jokes,
and daily updates.
Promises of flying me to Washington to see him.
I could hardly wait.
He would leave her and send me my ticket.
But I never got on that plane, did I?
I was just there to help him pass the time.
A little bit of home
to keep him connected
and entertained.
He never meant it to be more,
did he?
That became painfully clear
when he married her.
Does she know about the emails?
Does she know how we spoke to each other?
Does he have deep discussions

and make jokes with her
the way he did with me?
She looks a little bit like me,
doesn't she?
When he thinks back to his days training overseas,
does he think about me?
When he drinks Jameson,
does he remember that night?
It's all a dream I had to wake up from.

Wallis Sands

We walked the beach looking for seashells.
Big or small.
All shapes and sizes.
If we were lucky,
we'd find some sea glass
to add to her collection.
But it wasn't about what we were looking for.
It was about you and her.
The way she looked up at you
and grabbed your hand.
You could tell
she really loved you.
She loved you like
dipping toes in the cold ocean water,
finding Easter eggs hidden under the porch,
pink fingernail polish,
waiting for Santa on Christmas Eve,
gray and yellow Flagler tee shirts,
Panera flip flop cookies,
chasing seagulls,
and blowing bubbles in the backyard.
A love that was just yours and hers.
But summer came and went,
and we searched the sands without you.
We added to her collection,
but it wasn't about what we were looking for.
It was about what we were missing.

Mount Vernon Variety

Time is irrelevant.
Has it been one day?
One week?
Or an entire year?
It feels like yesterday.
It always feels like yesterday with you.
No matter how much time passes,
you are you
and I am me.
Forever 17 and 19.
Stuck in a time capsule,
drinking a cotton candy slush,
eating Bomb Pops and
chocolate band-aids,
driving along the coastline
until we get to watch the fireworks.
Maybe we'll stop at Tripoli's for a slice
or Joe's Playland
to play "Dream a Dream."
But it doesn't matter what we do.
You are you
and I am me.
Time is irrelevant.
So I'll see you in one day
or one week
or sometime next year.
And it will feel just like yesterday.

My Mother's Line

It didn't just happen to me,
it happened to her too.
Everything I've experienced,
she experienced too.
In a different way
and in the same way.
All our experiences are intertwined,
determined before we were born,
written into our histories
almost like we couldn't escape it.
It didn't start with what she did to me,
or even what her mother did to her,
but with generations
down our family line.
Mothers try to get it right,
but it only turns out wrong.
We try not to repeat past mistakes,
only to make new ones.
We try to close the cuts and wounds,
put a bandage on them,
and call ourselves healed.
But are we really?
We go around fixing everyone else.
After all, it's our job to take care of others,
forgetting about ourselves.
But generation after generation,
mothers have daughters,
and daughters become mothers.
A forever cycle of getting it wrong.
Maybe one day we'll get it right.
Can I get it right for her?

The First Sip

From the moment it hit my lips,
I was hooked.
I knew it was going to be a problem.
It took my worries and anxieties away.
Trauma was forgotten
and replaced with a charisma I didn't know I had.
I began to look forward to the weekends,
to weeknights,
then to every day after class.
Soon my charisma transformed
into crying in the corner,
no longer the life of the party.
Just the sad girl
always on the verge of blacking out.
There are so many holes in my memory.
Maybe it's better that I don't remember.
I put myself in dangerous situations,
my fate left to the will of others.
I woke up in places I did not recognize.
But it wasn't a problem,
I'd tell myself.
I'd lie to myself.
Just one more sip,
on one more night,
and everything would be alright.
The thoughts and flashbacks would stop.
I wouldn't feel anything.
I wouldn't remember anything.
Just me and the bottle
drowning everything out.
I'd take a drink and close my eyes,
and everything would be alright.

Happiness?

I could have loved him forever.
That was my plan.
We built a life,
and I was proud of it.
But somewhere along the way,
I cracked
and I broke
and I became rotten.
A person I don't recognize.
I can't even remember before.
Happiness?
I don't even know that word.
It's a foreign language
or a suppressed memory
right on the tip of my tongue.
I can almost taste it.
But it vanishes
and I'm left with nothing.
I continue to stumble and tumble,
trying to get my footing.
Trying to land where I was before.
I'm in a place I do not recognize,
looking at a stranger's reflection.

Venus de Milo

I am a sculpture.
Little pieces of me are chipped away.
The artist keeps chipping with his hammer and chisel.
Chip, chip, chip
until there is barely anything left.
There is nothing left for me
but broken shards and dust scattered on the floor.
Remnants of what used to be,
while my artist works on his next piece of marble.
Maybe she won't be worn down,
but pristinely kept,
looked at,
and admired by those passing by.
She's perfect
and bright
and new
while my pieces lie on the floor,
scattered and forgotten.
Soon those pieces will be picked up off the floor.
By onlookers and those passing by.
Pieces I needed to remain whole.
People always take and rarely give.
I hope what they took
was worth it in the end,
as my remnants of dust
are swept away.

Birthday Balloons

I thought this day would be different.
33.
But it's more of the same.
He took me back to my apartment
and I stumbled up the stairs.
He was on top of me
and everything was hazy.
He rolled me over
and took what wasn't his.
Another he said/she said.
It's almost like my voice
doesn't matter anymore.
Men take what they want
and leave me with nothing.
Is anybody listening?
Can anybody hear me?
Left in my bed,
in the dark,
I can hear him leaving my apartment,
starting his car.
Driving away
with my balloons still in his backseat.

Ruby Grapefruit

He cracked open the can
and handed it to me,
after I politely refused three times.
One sip turned into two sips
which turned into another
and another.
I'd worked hard on my sobriety,
and it ended with him.
I just couldn't say no,
there was just something about him.
So charismatic and charming,
uncomfortably attractive.
I would do anything to please him,
all he had to do was ask.
We shared a few nights like this.
It was slightly less satisfactory
for me than it was for him,
but still I kept coming back
and back and back.
Time passed without a word
until he was alone again.
He was bored so he called me,
because he knew I would answer.
But all he could say
were endless comparisons.
How I was better.
How I was sweeter.
How I was more affectionate.
But he didn't pick me,
he picked her.
Now she's gone,
and I still have not been chosen.
"We have so much wasted time

to make up for," he said.
"I wish you could spend the night."
We'd never done that.
He assumed that I couldn't,
which is why he offered.
When I told him I could,
he stumbled to find an excuse.
But I didn't listen.
I lay in my own bed alone
and realized I was the one
who had wasted time.

Her

Little webs in doorway corners.
Darkness hides her secret intentions.
She spins her web
with a perfect string of silk.
Lying in wait
until fate sways in her favor.
She catches her flies
and sucks them till she's ready
to discard their empty shells.
Then she'll blame them
for their own misfortune.
How many will be enough?
She lies in wait
for her next victim
to find their way into her silk sheets.
Does she tell them their time is ending
before she sinks in her fangs?
Or does that take away
from the pleasure of the hunt?
When she catches me,
will she release me?
Or will she strike once I'm lying
comfortably under
the covers she spun just for me?

An Education

I sat there on the carpet.
It was meticulous.
I could still see the perfect lines,
straight and in order.
Not a thread out of place.
He pressed play on the VHS
and I waited
for my continued education.
Groomed like the carpet.
I would be perfect—
his favorite.
The video came into focus.
It was about a little family,
just like mine.
Picture perfect.
She looked a little bit like me,
didn't she?
I knew what would happen before
the scene came on the screen.
They sat on the bench.
A "happy ending" with his coffee.
He liked his black, didn't he?
I understood.
I would be perfect.
Straight and in order.
Not a thread out of place.
Did I do a good job, daddy?
Am I still your favorite?
Your goldmine?
When will my next lesson be?
I need to continue my education.

"You're Ruining Your Life"

It was like walking a tightrope.
I would slowly walk across
without looking ahead.
I'd close my eyes and feel the rope sway me
from side to side.
Left to right.
To live or to die.
I would go wherever fate decided,
not caring either way.
Soon I could feel myself
edging more to the right.
I became reckless,
careless and frivolous.
I stopped walking the rope
and stood waiting to fall.
I continuously put myself
in dangerous situations.
Situations that would do the job for me.
That didn't work
so I started to walk faster
until finally I reached the end of the rope.
But fate forgot that I held the knife
in my hand.
I was done waiting for someone
or something to push me over.
You can't ruin your life
when you have nothing left to lose.
So I stood on the rope,
playing with my knife.
Waiting for the perfect moment
to make the cut.

Family Ties

It started off as an empty bin.
Slowly it began to fill
with leftover TV dinners,
half-eaten birthday cake,
pristine plates left untouched.
The food was fresh but soon became rotten.
The smell of decay started to take over.
It infected everyone
so no one was safe. If you tried
to protect yourself, you were
ridiculed and ostracized.
The food was tainted—
it couldn't be at fault.
You had to adjust, make the environment
less hostile. Make it more comfortable,
risking your own safety.
Eventually you realized
this wasn't a way to live.
It was time to take out the trash.

Latibule

She is like sunshine,
beaming at me with all of her rays.
Giving me the light and warmth I need to survive.
When dusk falls and she slips past the horizon,
she makes sure the moon comes out just for me.
So I will always have a light to guide my path.
I am safe because I know she is with me.
Every time I take a step, she takes one too.
With her I will never walk alone.
She is my shadow scaring away the crows.
She leaves her footprints behind
so I can trace my steps back.
Back to my garden where I am safe and sound,
where the flowers bloom because she gives them what they need.
My lilacs are the perfect shade of purple
and my ivy climbs the fences.
We sit on the bench in the garden we created,
breathing in the air, finally at peace.

About the Author

Meghan A. Patricia Wentworth is a writer from Portsmouth, New Hampshire currently living in Dover. She wrote her first poem, "This House," as a way to help her heal from the multitude of trauma she experienced at the time. She decided to share it at an open mic in front of fifty strangers, and it received a standing ovation. That level of validation gave her the strength and encouragement to continue her writing journey and "Stay Until Tomorrow," her debut book of poetry, was born.

Acknowledgments

"The Secret Garden" and "Him" were previously published in the anthology *On an Unpleasant Note* (Poet's Choice, November 2024).

"Peirce Island" appears in the 2025 issue of *The Heron*, the literary magazine at Great Bay Community College.

First, I'd like to thank Samantha Kolber, and the entire team at Rootstock Publishing. Your dedication and belief in me are absolutely everything. The guidance, patience, and the care you have shared with me and my words is beyond my expectations. You gently unearthed my traumas and kept them safe as I began to share them with the world. For that, I am forever thankful.

For RW, we built a beautiful life, side by side. Just because it ended, doesn't mean it wasn't worth every single second. I am incredibly proud of where we are and how we've handled it with such grace. She is first and foremost the reason for everything. We have managed to make the best of our heartbreak in the hopes that she remains unscathed. Our hearts beat for her and I am so thrilled ours have the same rhythm. I will always be thankful for you.

For M, you came into my life when you needed me and I needed you. I wanted you forever but fate and time had other plans. Every single moment with you were the best moments of my life. I think of you every second of every day. We never get enough time but it's because of you that I am this strong. You gave me the strength I needed to make this book a reality. I'll meet you at the park in my dreams, my little Moose. When I close my eyes, we are there. A place for us to swing, laugh and play for hours. Finally together again.

For BH, you didn't get to choose me but I was a package deal with B. I know I can be hard to love but you love me anyways. I look for you always. At dinners, weddings and family reunions. Your support and love knows no bounds. I am more thankful for you then you will ever know. I love you one hundred dollars.

I can't give enough thanks to AK. She read every single poem, even before they were done. When they were coarse, rough and raw. Pebbles that would soon become a mountain. Calls at midnight were never unanswered. You are my kindred spirit, my other half. You took the time and energy to hike up to the peak with me. Now we can sit and enjoy the view.

To those of you who find yourselves in these words, I can't help but feel slightly grateful. Every trauma, life lesson and person who has come into my life, have caused a ripple effect. Some of the waves are ever so small and others are like tsunamis. I am thankful that you have helped teach me how to swim. Now, it's almost like I don't even need a life vest. I can swim safely to the shore alone. When I finally land on the beach, I will lay in the sand and soak in the rays. Healed, whole and unbroken.

And, of course, I am thankful for you, my reader. You have kept me going. The thought that I am able to express these tragedies with you is not lost on me. I hope you read them with a tender eye and are able to keep them locked away for yourself. That they may help you feel validated, heard and not so alone. If you need a life vest, you can have mine. I will help you swim to the shore. You are always welcome to bask in the sunlight with me.

🌱 We Grow Our Books in Montpelier, Vermont

Learn more about our titles in Fiction, Nonfiction, Poetry and Children's Literature at the QR code below or visit www.rootstockpublishing.com.

www.ingramcontent.com/pod-product-compliance
Lightning Source LLC
Chambersburg PA
CBHW020443090526
44586CB00045B/807